Gospel Favorites for Solo Ukulele

by Joe Carr

I0901686

Online Audio

www.melbay.com/30027BCDEB

Audio Contents

Track #		Track #	
1	Tuning	15	Just a Closer Walk With Thee
2	Abide with Me	16	Life's Railway to Heaven
3	Amazing Grace	17	Nearer My God to Thee
4	Are You Washed in the Blood?	18	Oh Mary, Don't You Weep
5	Down By the Riverside	19	Oh Sinner Man
6	Farther Along	20	Old Rugged Cross
7	God of Our Fathers	21	Onward Christian Soldiers
8	Have a Little Talk With Jesus	22	Pass Me Not
9	I Am a Pilgrim	23	Power in the Blood
10	In the Garden	24	Rock of Ages
11	In the Sweet By and By	25	Shall We Gather at the River?
12	Jacob's Ladder	26	Standing in the Need of Prayer
13	Jesus Loves the Little Children	27	Softly and Tenderly
14	Jesus Loves Me		

Special thanks to Gerald Jones for his playing on the companion audio. Tenor ukulele by Joe Mendel of Mendel Fretted Instruments, Chesterf eld, MO.

1 2 3 4 5 6 7 8 9 0

Visit us on the Web at www.melbay.com — E-mail us at email@melbay.com

Contents

Gospel Favorites for Solo Ukulele

The ukulele is used most often as a rhythm instrument to accompany singing. The infectous rhythm produced by the ukulele provides an attractive background for sing-alongs. The ukulele is also an effective solo instrument carrying both the melody and chords when playing specially arranged music. In the 1920s and 30s, a number of genius string wizards including Roy Smeck and George Formby demonstrated the "uke's" ability to produce a full sound all by itself.

This book includes 26 classic gospel favorites arranged for solo ukulele. These tunes come from the rich palette of hymns, songs and spirituals in the Christian tradition. These arrangements sound wonderful played by musicians of all levels. Some arrangements are suited to beginners while others will be best played by more advanced players. Regardless of your previous experience, these arrangements, even played at slow tempos, will produce an attractive full sound.

Each arrangement includes guitar chords that can be played as accompaniment. The given music is correct for soprano, concert and tenor ukuleles tuned in the re-entrant style to G C E A. This music can be played on baritone ukulele also, but the music will sound in a different key and the guitar chords will not be correct.

Re-entrant refers to the order of notes in the standard "my dog has fleas" ukulele tuning. Instead of ascending low to high, the uke tuning begins with a G note followed by a lower C note. If a player chooses to replace the fourth string with a thicker string and tune it to the G one octave lower than normal, this is referred to as "low G" tuning and the uke tuning then is no longer considered re-entrant. This is a possible but less common way to tune the uke.

These arrangements are designed so that the melody note is either a solo note or the last note of the chord when strummed from the fourth string to the first. Careful tuning is an important part of achieving a good sound. Use audio track 1 to get in good tune before each playing session. If you prefer to use a keyboard, tune the strings to G C E A (Green Cows Eat Apples.) For experienced guitarists, these strings are like the 4th through 1st strings of the guitar capoed at the 5th fret. Alternately, the familiar tune "my dog has fleas" can be used to tune if no standard note source is available. When using this "by ear" method, be careful that the C string is not too loose (bad sound) and the A string is not too tight (it may break.)

Track 1

Abide with Me

Track 2

Amazing Grace

Track 3

Are You Washed in the Blood?

Track 4

Down By the Riverside

Track 5

D
A
17
E
A
21
D
A
25
E
A
29

Farther Along

Track 6

God of Our Fathers

Track 7

Have a Little Talk With Jesus

Track 8

17
E
A
21
D
A
25
F♯m
E
A
D
A
29

I Am a Pilgrim

Track 9

In the Garden

Track 10

In the Sweet By and By

Track 11

Jacob's Ladder

Track 12

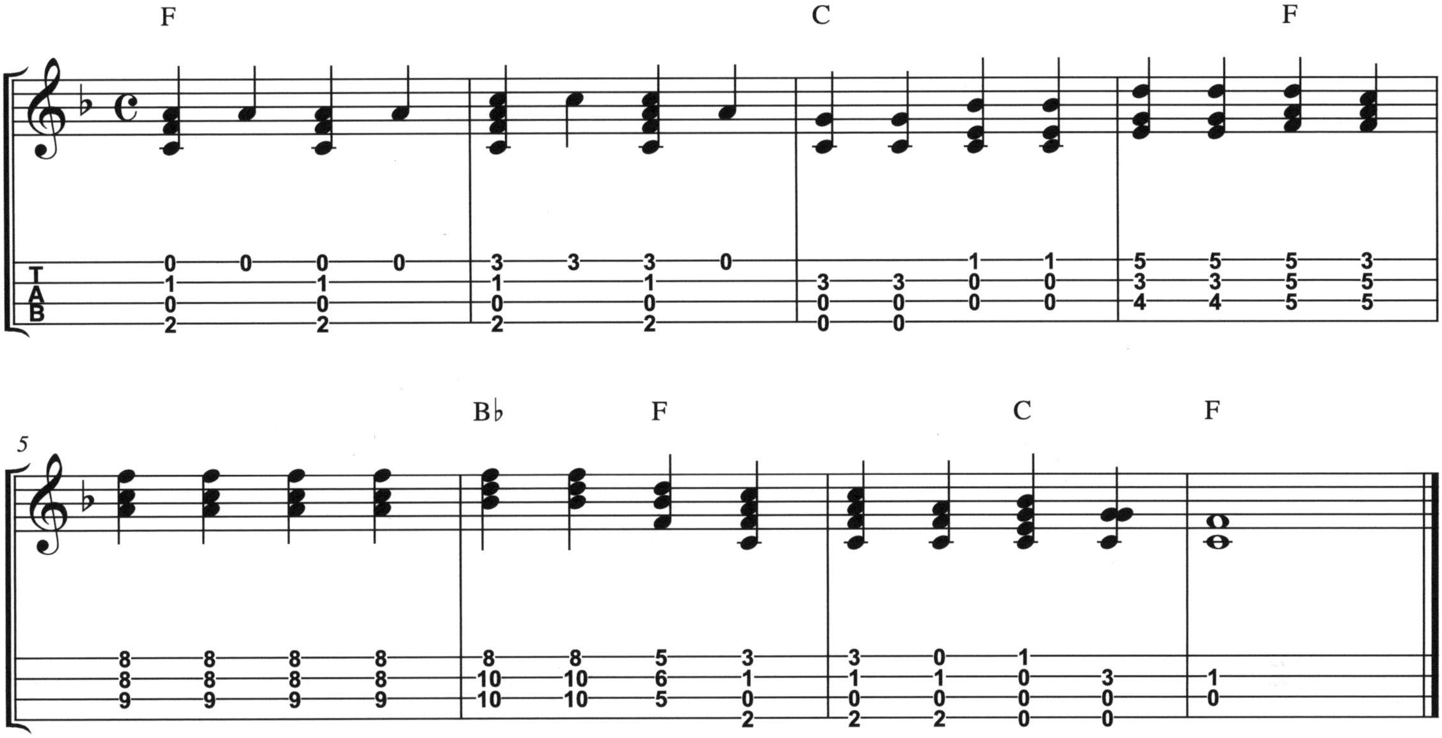

Jesus Loves the Little Children

Track 13

Jesus Loves Me

Track 14

Just a Closer Walk with Thee

Track 15

Life's Railway to Heaven

Track 16

24
E7 A D A
30
E7 A
36
D A E7 A
42

Nearer My God to Thee

Track 17

Oh Mary, Don't You Weep

Track 18

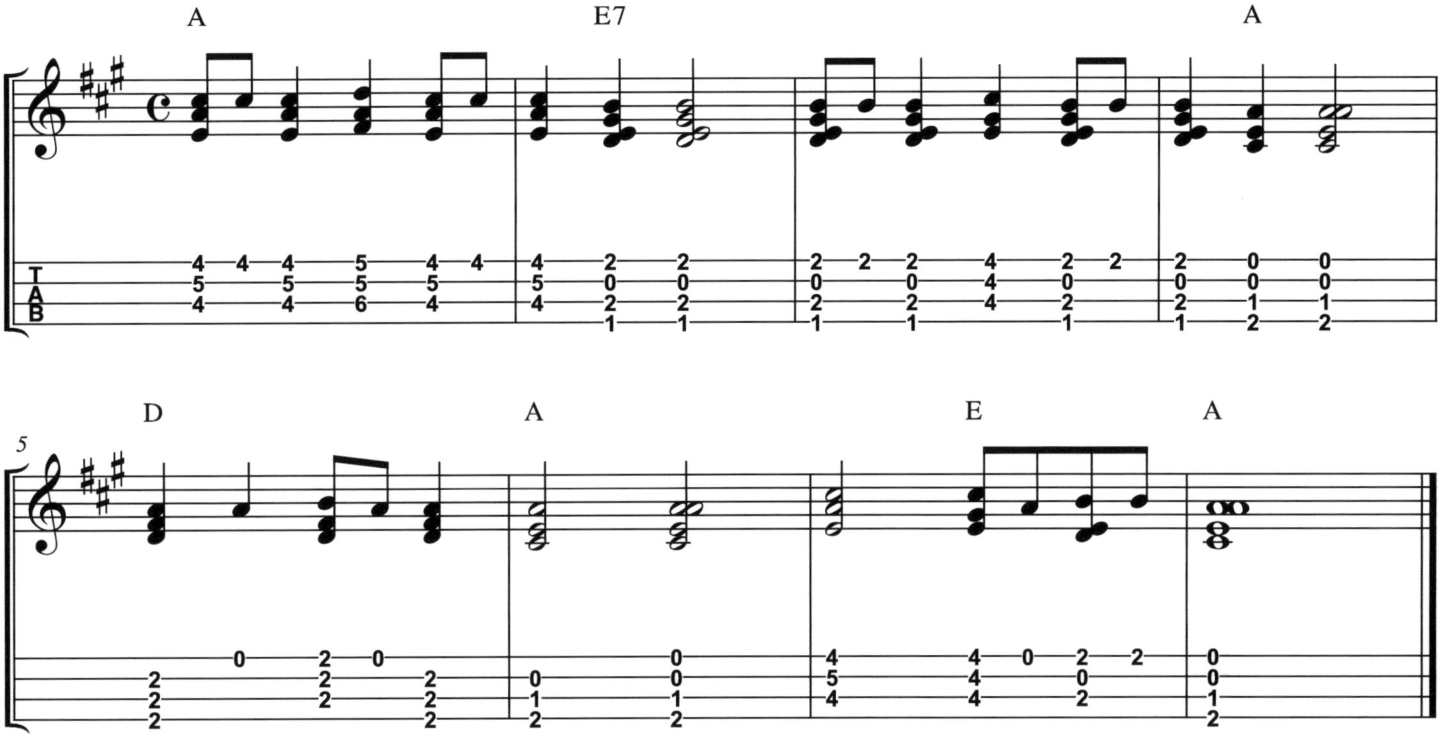

Oh Sinner Man

Track 19

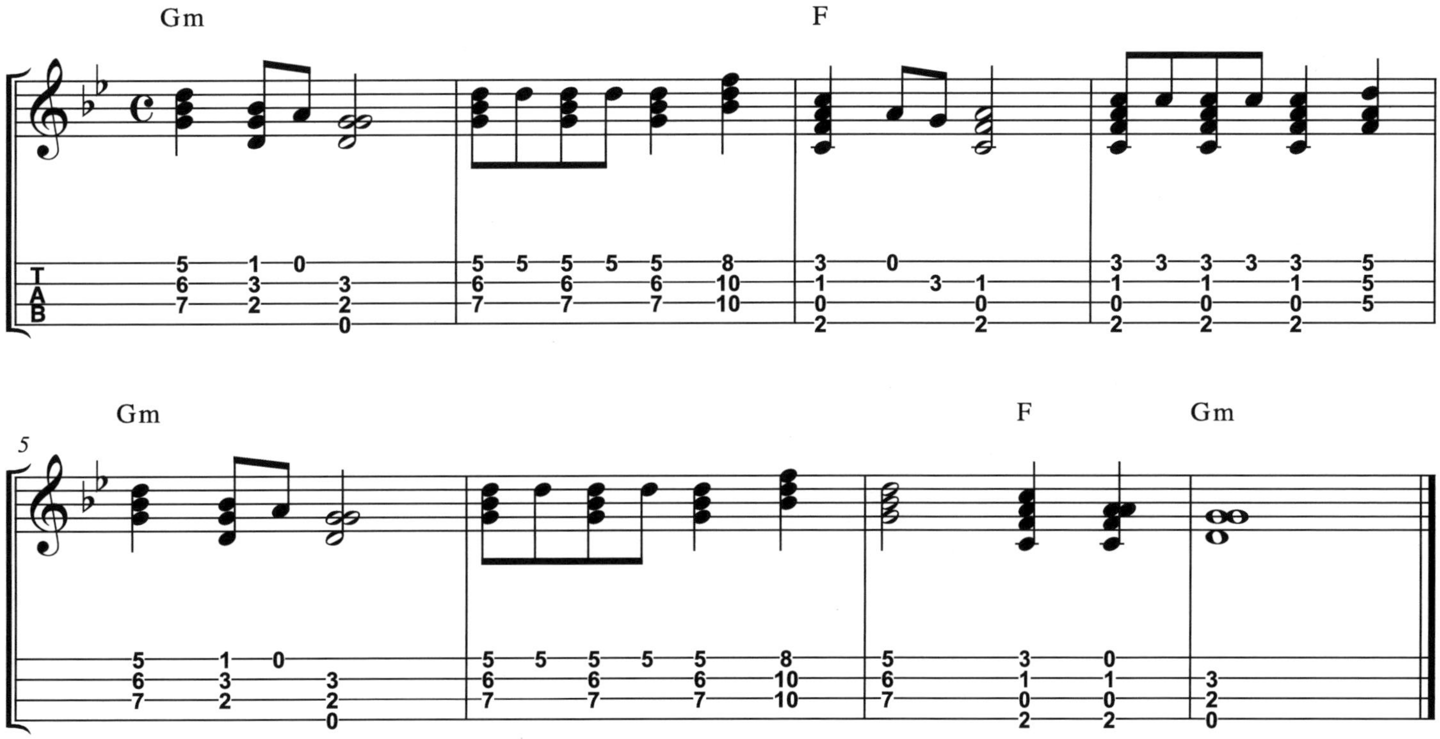

Old Rugged Cross

Track 20

16
G
C
20
F
G
25
C
F
29
C
G
C

Onward Christian Soldiers

Track 21

Pass Me Not

Track 22

Power in the Blood

Track 23

Rock of Ages

Track 24

Shall We Gather at the River?

Track 25

Standing in the Need of Prayer

Track 26

Softly and Tenderly

Track 27

17
E
A
21
B
E
E7
25
A
A+
D
A
29
F♯m
E
A
D
A

Conclusion

Congratulations! By completing this volume you are well on your way to making your ukulele playing a complete melody and rhythm style. Pick a good ukulele key and try arranging your favorite melodies. A simple internet search will reveal the broad range of songs people are trying out on the uke. While most people use the ukulele only as an accompaniment to their singing, you are now prepared to try to play the melody and chords.

Be sure to look for other ukulele books by the same author including "Folk Songs for Solo Ukulele" (MB30026M) and "Holiday Favorites for Solo Ukulele" (MB30028M) I would like to acknowledge several Internet based gospel song books, especially Cyher Hymnal, for their help as a resource for correct titles, melodies and historical information.

About the Author

Since 1985, Joe Carr has been a music instructor specializing in Bluegrass, Western Swing and Irish music in the Commercial Music program at South Plains College in Levelland, Texas. He is the director for Camp Bluegrass, a summer residential music camp in its 26th year (2012.)

In 1977, Joe joined the internationally known *Country Gazette* bluegrass band with banjo player Alan Munde and bluegrass legend Roland White. Joe appeared on three group albums, a solo album and numerous other recorded projects during his seven-year tenure with the band. In the 1990s, Carr and Munde formed a duo that toured extensively throughout the U.S., Canada and England and recorded two albums for Flying Fish/Rounder Records.

Joe has developed and appeared in over thirty instructional music videos for Mel Bay Publications and Texas Music & Video. He has written many instructional book/audio combinations for Mel Bay and has a growing number of DVDs available. Included are diverse titles such as *Western Swing Fiddle* MB20289M, *Mandolin Gospel Tunes* MB20554M and *School of Country Guitar* MB21645M.

Joe is a regular columnist for *Flatpicking Guitar Magazine and Mandolin Magazine*. In 1996, the Texas Tech University Press published *Prairie Nights to Neon Lights: The Story of Country Music in West Texas* by Carr and Munde. Joe can be seen and heard at acousticmusician.com/JoeCarr.html He plays Mendel ukuleles.

In 2008, Joe received the International Bluegrass Music Association's Distinguished Achievement award.